WORDS OF GRATITUDE

Inspiring and Encouraging
Poems About God From the Heart

Michelle Mitchell

Words of Gratitude: Inspiring and Encouraging Poems
About God From the Heart

Copyright © 2023 by Michelle Mitchell

First Edition

Pure Thoughts Publishing, LLC

www.purethoughtspublishing.com

Brief news excerpts, public statements, and images by individuals or companies other than the author are used under section 107 of the copyright act 1976; allowance is made for "fair use" for purposes such as criticism, commentary, news reporting, teaching, scholarship, and research.

No part of this book may be reproduced in whole or in part, stored in a retrieval system, or transmitted in any form, or by any means, electronic, mechanical, photocopying, recording, or otherwise, without prior permission of the author, except by a reviewer, who may quote brief passages in a review.

ISBN: 978-1-953760-27-2

All rights reserved.

Table of Contents

Thanks for Another Chance 5

Always Right There 8

Thanks to God's Grace 10

Receive It!! 13

Present Help 15

God Deserves Praise 17

On Time God 19

Love Anyway 21

Nothing Is Impossible 23

Pray 25

He Will Restore 26

Stay Strong 27

Everything Will Be Okay 28

We Are Blessed 29

Stay Focused 31

You're My Everything 33

Believe 34

Prepare For Blessings 36

You'll Be Just Fine 38

Be Happy 40

It's Already Done 41

Scripture: 42

Picture 43

About the Author: 44

Thanks for Another Chance

Some go about life
hoping for the best.
Some forget it's our
faith God will test.

It's something on which
God will never rest.
Having faith is something
that God will suggest.

Having faith, no matter
what is God's protest.
Trusting in him always
is what he'll request.

Some get in accidents
while others get ill.
Emptiness in them is
what God will fill.

Making us feel better
is God's powerful skill.
Our life is something
that God will fulfill.

Whatever you have survived
be thankful about it.
Survival and everlasting favor
are things he'll permit.

To God is whom
we should always commit.
With God always alongside
we should never quit.

Being thankful for surviving
is something to admit.
Regardless, to God is
whom we should submit.

Be grateful for that
second chance in life.
No matter what you've
been through even strife.

Say, "thanks for another
chance" which will arrive.

God's mercy for us
he will never deprive.

Always Right There

All of my life
you've been beside me.
Making sure your love
is what I see.

It's not always I
instead, it's always we.
With your protection I'm
always safe and free.

Your love and protection
is always a guarantee.
That is something of
with I can't disagree.

Because you are there,
I am not afraid.
That is something of
which I won't trade.

Closeness existed before the
price your son paid.
And it lasts forever
and will never fade.

Because you are there,
I do not worry.
When fellowshipping, I am
never in a hurry.

Of praise is what
you are truly worthy.
I see your words
and I meditate early.

I don't waste time
on our wonderful journey.
Because you are there,
I really don't worry.

Gratefully, with you by
me, I'm never lonely.
It is clear that
you are no phony.

You are the one
I will worship only.
You're always right there
and won't disown me.

Thanks to God's Grace

No one is perfect,
but that doesn't matter
and we are blessed;
thanks to God's grace.

Some may have sinned
and they are forgiven
and will always be;
thanks to God's grace.

Some may not put
God first, but he
will love them anyway;
thanks to God's grace.

There are some that
were in an accident,
but they made it;
thanks to God's grace.

Others may feel they
may not get a
job, but doors open;
thanks to God's grace.

Some may have been
struggling in school, but
they managed to graduate;
thanks to God's grace.

Some may be going
through a divorce, but
God mended their relationship;
thanks to God's grace.

Bickering may be a
norm in some households,
but it can be fixed;
thanks to God's grace.

Illness may be the
only thing some know,
but they are healed;
thanks to God's grace.

Struggling with identity may
be common, but surely
not for too long;
thanks to God's grace.

Give thanks and approbation
to God, because there
are things made possible;
thanks to God's grace.

Receive It!!

Sickness is everywhere and
diseases are a norm.
In countless different ways,
they develop and form.

God is the answer
and is our reform.
Healing is something that
he will always perform.

He makes sure that
we're safe and warm.
He can control the
sun and a storm.

Some may feel hopeless
and like they're lacking.
It is blessings that
God is already stacking.

It is doubt that
people should start unpacking.
That enemy at times
can be very distracting.

Remember that God will
always make a way.
Forget about what the
enemy has to say.

The Lord is in
charge of every day.
He will take sickness
and those diseases away.

People that need healing
just need to pray.
Sickness and diseases may
come, but won't stay.

Be joyful about deliverance
and do not pout.
Know that God will
always work things out.

That is the truth
and do not doubt.
Have gratitude, receive it,
and sing and shout.

Present Help

Almost everyone has struggled
and reached their limit.
Some feel like giving
up at any minute.

Some let hardship and
tribulations hinder their spirit.
Remember, God isn't around
for a short visit.

With God, trust no
matter what is implicit.
That is something that
we should not prohibit.

Sometimes our days and
nights can be grim.
And our chances of
victory seem very slim.

That's the perfect time
to trust in him.
We shouldn't let the
light inside us dim.

Life sometimes makes people
feel powerless and stuck.
Some may feel like
they have bad luck.

Some feel on them
that lightening has struck.
And yes, struggling and
hard times really suck.

The negative thoughts are
what we should pluck.
Under our covers it
is us he'll tuck.

It is true that
he will never leave.
That is something we
should accept and receive.

Be in gratitude of
God and always believe.
He's present help and
our tribulations he'll relieve.

God Deserves Praise

Numerous things happen in
the world we live.
Some lie and cheat
while others don't forgive.

Some don't know it's
mercy God will give.
It is us that
the enemy will misgive.

We must always remember
our faith will outlive.
And the enemy's failure
is something he'll relive.

God does a lot
for all of us.
God will never throw
us under the bus.

He gives grace and
that is a plus.
For that we should
not make a fuss.

God is our everything
and that is true.
Some people don't know
and have no clue.

God does a lot
for me and you.
There's hardly anything that
we need to do.

He really makes our
skies clear and blue.
He takes away shame
from the unholy too.

We should express gratitude
with praise to him.
The light inside us
he will not dim.

Getting to know our
Father is not grim.
God deserves praise always
overflowing from the brim.

On Time God

Some are in need
of a way out;
trying to find relief,
but they have doubt.

Faith is what they
lack and are without.
They need to give
God praise and shout.

They need to trust
God and not pout.
During struggle is when
faith will really count.

When you trust God,
things will get better.
God makes no mistakes
and makes no error.

God always comes through
and loves you forever.
God will always help
you get things together.

Know that God will
always be with you.
Know that for everything
he will come through.

Situations may get tough
and that is true.
But God is always
our way maker too.

No matter, he always
makes our skies blue.
For this, praise and
worship is always due.

God is an on
time God for all.
Have gratitude that he's
there before you fall.

On him, we should
never hesitate to call.
God helps our situations
whether big or small.

Love Anyway

There are people that
are filled with hate.
Their actions are on
time and never late.

An uncomfortable space is
what they always create.
Of course, things like
that are not great.

Regardless, God knows how
to set things straight.
He will correct those
hateful people just wait.

For those people he
uses tenderness and care.
Those are the things
 that we should share.

It can make a
difference no matter where.
Those two things are
honest, just, and fair.

When people treat you
wrong, don't get mad.
When people say harmful
things, don't be sad.

When someone is hurtful
towards you, be glad.
Stay positive and trust
it's not that bad.

Make them want the
love you've always had.
A lifestyle in their
life they could add.

Be grateful that God
will always love anyway.
Imitate God and love
today and every day.

Let people know that
to love is okay.
Show this in the
actions that you portray.

Nothing Is Impossible

Situations in life can
be complicating for some.
That is when tests
and hard times come.

Sometimes these situations can
make you feel numb;
without energy and the
more secluded you become.

Don't forget that God
always knows the outcome.
And there's nothing to
which God will succumb.

God can take feelings
of being overwhelmed away.
His help is what
he will not delay.

Remember that God always
has the final say.
He can really turn
your night into day.

Whether jobless, homeless or
feeling useless always believe.
With God, there is
nothing you won't achieve.

Make efforts to pray
and prepare to receive.
It is his children
that he will relieve.

It is the enemy
that will always deceive.
But God makes a
way and won't leave.

Nothing is impossible for
God and it's true.
During hard times, he
knows what to do.

For this we should
all be in gratitude.
Regardless, God can make
things possible for you.

Pray

There are a lot
of hardships people face.
Some feel like they're
in a perpetual race.

They are far away
from their own pace.
And some feel like
they're out of place.

That's when you and
God will need space.
Prayer is the most
important in this case.

No matter what you
go through just pray.
Believe that the hard
times will not stay.

Know that God will
always make a way.
Be in gratitude of
prayer always including today.

He Will Restore

Experiencing good and bad
times have happened anyway.
You can't avoid it
whether night or day.

Some feel there's nothing
to do or say.
Nothing to make those
bad times go away.

Remember, even at your
worst, God will stay.
During life's problems, he
will make a way.

Be in gratitude that
he'll make things right.
He will restore and
make our days bright.

At the end of
the tunnel there's light.
Of God, during restoration,
we shouldn't lose sight.

Stay Strong

Life has its way
of changing our perspective.
When things get complicated,
people sometimes become aggressive.

Some attack people they
love and play detective.
Trying to figure out
things while being protective.

They guard their heart
and suddenly become rejective.
Refusing God's help not
knowing this isn't effective.

Regardless of the situation
you're in be sturdy.
Have gratitude God gives
strength and don't worry.

Weakness exists, but don't
give it the glory.
Stay strong regardless knowing
that is your story.

Everything Will Be Okay

When growing up, some
encounter situations and trouble.
Life's circumstances seem to
make their life tumble.

Bickering and mourning happen
and they encounter struggle.
Some want to just
stay in a bubble.

Some people think that
they are seeing double.
Sometimes circumstances repeat even
when they are humble.

No matter the trouble
that comes just pray.
Have gratitude that you'll
always see another day.

"Thank God" is something
you should always say.
Know without a doubt
everything will be okay.

We Are Blessed

Sometimes some feel like
all hope is lost.
Some think that they
have paid the cost.

They're waiting for a
break someone will toss.
They feel there's no
help and that's false.

Little do they know
God is the boss.
So is Christ who
died on the cross.

So many things are
in store for us.
It may seem impossible,
but just always trust.

Trust that with God
there is no distrust.
Know that in everything
God is always just.

He will always give
us what we need.
We can trust in
him with everything indeed.

For grace, we do
not have to plead.
For blessings, we just
have to always believe.

Because Christ died for
our sins, we're freed.
When blessings come say
"It's something I'll receive."

We should be grateful
and know we're blessed.
Believe that with God
you won't be distressed.

God has things in
store for us regardless.
Trusting that we are
blessed is his request.

Stay Focused

There are countless things
we do every day.
Work and school occupy
us come what may.

Challenges make it seem
success is far away.
Some forget to take
the time to pray.

Some forget that God
will make a way;
even when you're left
with nothing to say.

Even when you feel
things won't work out;
remember, learn not to
get distracted by doubt.

Do not shy away
from the positive route.
Remember always remain positive,
motivated, and encouraged throughout.

That is what God
wants you to be.
All of these things
are costless and free.

They're freely given if
only you could see.
Being able to have
them are a guarantee.

Blessings and favor are
what we should foresee.
That is something with
which God would agree.

Stay focused on God
and shine not dim;
your light inside knowing
that's far from grim.

Have gratitude that we
can concentrate on him.
That'll fill us with
joy to the brim.

You're My Everything

God you've done so
much and I agree.
It is your compassion
that I always see.

Because you sacrificed your
son, I am free.
The law of sin
will not bind me.

That is something with
which I won't disagree.
That freedom is something
that you'll always guarantee.

You are my freedom
and all I need.
I'm in gratitude that
it's me you'll lead.

Your strength and everything
I need to succeed.
You're my everything and
all I need indeed.

Believe

So many things are
up against us all.
Regardless, on God is
who we can call.

He will never leave
us nor forsake us.
Trusting in him is
something that's a must.

Some may feel they
want to give up.
They should know God
will fill their cup.

Bad things may happen,
but they won't last.
God is present help
regardless of our past.

God is always there
and right on time.
He helps us always
and during the climb.

We must have faith
no matter what happens.
We should trust him,
because he is our captain.

Why wouldn't we count
on God for anything?
Who he is should
make our hearts sing.

Be thankful for what
God has already done.
We have favor, because
of his only son.

Don't waiver and just
throw in the towel.
God is the one
we should not disavowal.

Have gratitude he makes
 a way and believe.
He is the one
that will never leave.

Prepare For Blessings

For the longest struggle
manages to come near.
When it does, some
get overwhelmed and fear.

Some get so worried
and shed a tear.
Everyone just wants all
their worries to disappear.

Never forget that to
God we are dear.
During hardship, that enemy
always tries to interfere;

tries to bring us
down, but just believe.
Believe and know that
God will never leave.

God's favor is there
for all to receive.
God always has something
great up his sleeve.

Don't let struggle or
fear bring you down.
God doesn't want us
to have a frown.

He gives us pastures
that won't turn brown.
We are blessed all
over from the crown.

Regardless, know that God
is always in town.
In our troubles, he
won't let us drown.

There is so much
that is in store.
Be grateful there's favor
knocking at our door.

Prepare for blessings and
know there's always more.
Know that with blessings
you will always soar.

You'll Be Just Fine

There are times when
hardship can come around.
Some feel help is
nowhere to be found.

It may feel as
if you are bound;
limited, stuck, and no
one makes a sound.

Nothing but you and
tears on the ground.
Know it is you
that God will surround.

Know that no matter
God will come through.
He will bring comfort
and peace to you.

Know that God will
make all things new.
He'll turn things around
if you never knew.

If you're struggling, God
will make a way.
Without a doubt, know
everything will be okay.

Look forward to prosperity
each and every day.
"I am blessed" is
something to always say.

With trust in God,
sickness will not stay.
Know your hardship and
struggle will pass away.

Be in gratitude that
things will work out.
Don't forget to give
God praise and shout.

Faith is something you
should never be without.
Know you'll be just
fine without a doubt.

Be Happy

Sometimes things go the
way we want it.
Other times things may
change just a bit.

During that change sometimes
hard times will hit.
And some want to
give in and quit.

The enemy takes our
joy if we permit.
Staying positive is something
of which to commit.

Staying positive about life
brings happiness and joy.
Have gratitude that is
from God to enjoy.

Be happy when the
enemy tries to annoy.
Annihilate his opportunities to
steal, kill, and destroy.

It's Already Done

Some may feel they
will never reach success.
Circumstances in life can
make them feel stress.

Know it is us
that God will bless.
It is true and
don't stay in distress.

It's our hard times
he will already address.
Our faith is something
we should always confess.

Be grateful and know
that we have won.
Know that our blessings
are already a ton.

Know that our victory
has definitely already begun.
God handled it and
know it's already done.

Scripture:

Psalm 28:7

The Lord is my strength and my shield;
my heart trusts in him, and he
helps me.
My heart leaps for joy,
and with my song I praise him.

That is a good reason to be grateful.

God Is Always Right There

About the Author:

I was born and raised in Los Angeles, California. I graduated from Los Angeles Southwest College in high school with an Associate Degree in Liberal Studies. In 2011, I got my high school diploma and received an Associate Degree all at the same time. I grew up moving from one place to another with my family. We were low income, so there were times when we could not afford certain things. It was by the grace of God that we were blessed with necessities like clothes, shoes, water, food, and other important things. Years ago, my two brothers, my mom and I were homeless and had to stay in a shelter for months. Although that was the case, I never complained. I knew that God had something up his sleeve for my mom, my brothers and me. We managed to move out of the shelter and finally have a place we can call ours. Since I was a little girl, I've always loved to write. Writing was a way of expressing my thoughts, how I feel, and what I believe. In middle school and high school, I wrote poems. I love to write about what God has done for me. There are many things that I am grateful for that God has done. I express that gratitude in my poems, and I would love to share them with the world.

www.ingramcontent.com/pod-product-compliance
Lightning Source LLC
Chambersburg PA
CBHW070749050426
42449CB00010B/2391